I MISS GETTING LOST

I MISS GETTING LOST

a *Yucatán Travelogue,*
via *Botched Haikus*

BY JULIO LUCERO

FIRST EDITION

Cover design, illustrations & typesetting by Barış Şehri *sehricoverdesign.com*

Library of Congress Cataloging-in-Publication Data has been applied for.

ISBN: 979-8-9906022-2-9

FOREWORD

This collection started as an attempt at haiku. However, once the juices began to flow, my muse and direction shifted. I found the mechanical five-seven-five form of haiku gratifying, though I caught myself veering away from the essence of traditional haiku. For instance, I found the concept of *kigo*, distinguishing seasons, to be redundant. Those who have been know the Yucatán is rarely anything but blistering hot summer.

It is not my intention to poke fun at haiku's elegant form; instead, I aim to create something playful and expressive. With that said, this collection is a blend of prose and verse, technically making it closer to senryu, and in some cases haibun, than it is to haiku. Knowing this up front will aid your enjoyment.

I Miss Getting Lost is a travelogue broken up into five sections. Each section represents a separate trip to the Yucatán, and therefore, a unique experience.

¡Adelante!

started with a girl
Mayan jungle, Palenque
wouldn't stop yapping

I'm not objecting
charm off the charts—a real hoot
her English accent

evening fire spinners
chorizo quesadillas
el Panchan, pure bliss

dry season, lustrous
wet season, chocolate milk
Agua Azul falls

cabaña mornings
howler monkey alarm clock
afternoon naps, snooze

bye-bye Palenque
what's good about Mérida?
eggs motuleños

los motuleños
second consecutive day
uff, can't get enough

bulging guidebooks
finger-tracing paper maps
pair of cats astray

sun-baked iguanas
chicharrón-skinned westerners
Chichén Itzá tours

boarded the ferry
camera out, pose, and snap
Isla Mujeres

hammocks, dangling feet
reggae rhythms in the background
typical hostel

checked our luggage
no singles available
communal lodging

first toes, knees, hips, waist
liquid turquoise, together
nos repegamos

stumbled back that night
unzip and unbutton, shhh
awkward frustration

traveling youngsters
life crammed into a backpack
two birds on a line

"is beach sex worth it?"
"not great as it sounds," she said
hell is granular

she went on and on
her friends were on Isla, too
bad first impression

second impression
lubricated by malbec
things went swimmingly

beach, day after day
sea's luscious lather, lost
we itch to migrate

all aboard the boat
a goodbye, final hug, bus
terminal silence

she goes south; I west
cleaved souls, nos extrañamos
we reunite, Belize

eight short years later
otra vez, otra chica
travel bug nibbles

Houston to Cancún
luggage fee, nickeled and dimed
you guessed it: Spirit

un colectivo
first stop Playa, then Tulum
ocean's balmy breath

lumpy pillows, fan
whirling bugs and mosquito
nets to the rescue

digital touchscreens
replace a vagabond's tome
lonelier planet

ruins on the water
Mayan ingenuity
hurricane test: passed

day trip to Cobá
sites connected by dirt trails
a bike ride away

overgrown temples
mossy steps, root-strangled stones
Mother Earth eats last

curious bipeds
turned courageous quadrupeds
Nohoch Mul's summit

"how is this legal?"
"anyone fallen before?"
pyramid crested

missed the last bus back
sat up front with taxista
discussing pibil

an educator
says it means "under the earth,"
"solo los pueblos"

mention Yucatán
people first think Mexico
really, it's Mayan

prendo las luces
cucaracha gigante
busco la chancla

geologist friends,
"Yucatán is like Swiss cheese"
unique formations

parched porous stone
filtered subterranean lakes
pristine cenotes

hotter than a dog
paddling with the turtles
Barton Springs echoes

"cold" not the right word
or maybe for a Texan
invigorating

well-behaved waves, froth
flat Fred Flintstone feet below
visibility

buoyant bobs and jumps
frolicking never gets old
my fingers, dates

beach walk with my girl
vast ocean of legs and thighs
eyes up, keep them up

crisp bed linens, air
conditioner and shampoo
la-di-da lodging

55

once again, Isla
mujer es diferente
no es lo mismo

as a kid, papá
constantly mentioned the coast
his dream retirement

he asked, He answered
dozens of condos later
fideicomiso

big word for "land trust"
law: coast reserved for Mexas
expat strategy

afternoon beach jaunt
dilapidated wood shed
"what is he selling?"

ice-cold coconuts
vigorous machete swings
fingers still intact

coconut water
add cinnamon, rum of course
los cocolocos

nectar of the gods
tree Gatorade, made boozy
kinda dangerous

strolling down the strip
"¡promoción! cerveza, ron..."
whispers, "weed, cocaine..."

"happens everywhere"
"back home, it's dangerous too"
people love to say

convo with papá
petty delinquency
"when you least expect…"

bird takes *shit* on shirt
random guys *help* clean the mess
wallet goes missing

moral of story:
no matter the location,
billfolds, front pocket!

discotecas roar
younger brother came prepared
Switch with controllers

joystick, buttons, smash
brothers stay in for the night
playing Nintendo

mustered up gumption
just two or three drinks, that's it
Tulum, here we come!

eco-chic, empty
thought this was up-and-coming
hopped to the next bar

waitress, "want free drinks?"
online review in exchange
not exactly free

slow morning, awake
from a boat in the distance
making choppy waves

cyan horizon
el mar manda saludos
ola, I wave back

"how do I do this?"
papá pulls from his cigar
"like a man, hijo"

"¿pulseras, chicles?"
"¿aventuras en lancha?"
¡déjame en paz!

seagulls and cast nets
every June, Port Aransas
reminiscences

school, careers, children
tradition on hiatus
our excuse: "busy"

two decades later
we bust out our calendars
time not found, but made

chit-chat in taxi
"¿qué piensas del Tren Maya?"
he wasn't too thrilled

montón de pesos
un ride, la ida nomás
el sindicato

ride-share forbidden
taxis corner the market
there's a word for that

la guardia nods
free to enter, fee to park
extra-loose wrist bands

resorts, not my style
quality family time
fuck it. *when in Rome*

oceanside service
margs, coladas, shrimp tacos
wallet hemorrhage

lounging by the sea
sand and styrofoam beads meld
deflated bean bags

people dash over
valiant turtle hatchlings
miracle of life

tourists intervene
"¡hijuesu...no las toques!"
tip of my tongue

locals know better
Tulum's crown jewel, turtles
nests are sectioned off

ray in the shallows
featherless wings graze over
the vegetation

young girl, door to door
"¿pulseras, aretes, chicle?"
adult waits outside

quaint souvenir shops
blocks of the same, uncommon
Mayan curios

looking for a deal?
regatear, meaning haggle
felines come to mind

manta button-up
one thousand seven hundred
"made in India"

who are they foolin'
million percent markup
too big for britches

note to mexiphiles:
when guayabera shopping,
go to Mérida

sister, cuñao, kids
mom, papá, bro had to work
nueva tradición

Houston layover
Tulum International
coming soon: concrete

economic growth
many players, few winners
story of LatAm

Tulum has options
please, reconsider Oxxo
local emphasis

western guilt runs deep
who am I to deny A/C?
my cold living room

mounds of tangled knots
some years are worse than others
raking sargazo

underneath Earth's grain
except head and wiggly toes
rosy, sun-kissed cheeks

kids go bananas
dusted off my camastro
salt rim, lick and sip

another goblet
too sweet, too much triple sec
quaffed two anyway

sea, fish, hummus, shrimp?
winkless toss-n-turn night, rash
ointment, Andantol

advice from my friends:
Pacific for mariscos,
Yucatán for pork

white shores of Tulum
ley: playa para todos
tall walls, mounted signs

locals at Playa
coarse asphalt ends, sand begins
I squint, Cozumel

uniforms and boots
armor from shoulder to shin
cherub-cheeked children

childhood memories
rods, tackle box, frozen squid
hired a fishing boat

caught three dorados
first fifteen minutes, no sweat
de volón pimpón

josh with fisherman
"queremos barracuda"
"pides al Señor"

barracuda, hooked!
papá wanted a monster
though small fish taste best

Tuesday salsa night
cover, open floor, live band
smiles: ear, teeth, ear

lady in blue dress
una bestia, danced it all
men hovered over

my hand extends, yes!
Lamborghini in high heels
too much car for me

suddenly, silence
congas, dazzling fire spinners
feels like Palenque

flames flicker and twirl,
younger self: it's party time!
older self: bedtime

airport-bound buses
empty, shameless manspreading
a victimless crime

daily departures
closer than I remember
nos vemos pronto

www.ingramcontent.com/pod-product-compliance
Lightning Source LLC
Chambersburg PA
CBHW020739130626
46554CB00006B/2054